PHASE 4 LIFE

Life's a Journey, Not a Diet

HEATHER JULIANI

Printed in the United States of America

ISBN: 9781494487607

You have brains in your head.
You have feet in your shoes.
You can steer yourself any direction you choose.
You're on your own, and you know what you know.
And you are the only one who'll decide where you'll go.
Dr. Seuss

CONTENTS

ACKNOWLEDGEMENTS

First and foremost I want to thank *you* for picking up this book and taking charge of your health and body! You are the reason I wrote this book in the first place, and I am so happy to guide you in your cooking and eating choices.

Thank you to my dear friends Colin and Jayne Watson who have been a constant source of motivation and encouragement in my life. We share the same beliefs about health, fitness, mind, body and spirit. You continually push me to do bigger and better things and to share my knowledge with others, as you have done. I love you both and am blessed to have you in my life.

I'd also like to thank my family and friends for always asking for my food recipes. I always said "I should write a book, "so this is for you!

And above all, thank you to my husband and best friend, Joe. We have grown so much through the years and been through all our diet mishaps together until we finally figured out what works to makes us both happier and healthier. I cherish the time we spend together, whether it's in the kitchen, working out or just hanging out. You are my best friend and I look forward to growing old with you. I love you more than anything in the world.

Joe has been so much a force in writing this book that I refer to "us" throughout the book, as it is "we" collectively who choose to share our cooking and eating habits with you.

INTRODUCTION

We are so excited for you that you are reading this book and care enough about yourself and your family to learn how to eat healthfully for the rest of your life.

You may have been there, we certainly have—trying every diet program around to "maybe this time" find what will work to lose weight and get your body in shape (or to *stay* in shape if you've already achieved the results you're after). You've tried phase after phase to no avail. STOP LOOKING! This is your **Phase 4 Life**—a way of living, not a diet, to carry you through life's journey, wherever great places it may take you.

Many people have the misconception that healthy equals boring, bland, flavorless, difficult… NOT SO! You'll not only have recipes as your guide, but we'll teach you how to make meals your own—to combine foods to make an original "your-name-here" meal and to actually enjoy the cooking process as well as the flavors of the meal. Most of the recipes can be made in 30 minutes or less, so "I don't have time to cook" is no excuse!

We are not chefs by profession, we have no formal cooking background, nor do we have a license in nutrition. However we know from over 20 years of experience on our own personal journeys, the challenges you will encounter in achieving and maintaining a healthy body.

We both grew up in the typical American family: our parents and siblings were never focused on nutrition or a regular, healthy eating plan; just good American food like hamburgers, pasta, bread and sandwiches, like most American families.

Joe played sports growing up, started working out at the gym as a teenager, and in his early 20's decided he wanted to get in shape for a body building competition. He was fanatical about his workouts as well as his diet and used some radical eating plans to achieve the desired body to win a show. Through diet coaches and trial and error, he learned what to eat, when to eat, and how much to eat to get his body show-ready. Some of the dieting and food choices were extreme, however. He once went so far as to smell a cookie, put another cookie in a plastic bag and chew it, just to get the feeling of eating a cookie without the calories; so he felt like he wasn't so deprived. Fortunately he realized that this was not a lifestyle or physique he could maintain on a day-to-day basis. Joe felt compelled to find an approach to food that could be followed for life after watching his sister struggle with her weight and his dad battle diabetes, which he later succumbed to.

I was never involved in sports or physical activities growing up. I was not athletic by any means, you might even say I was clumsy (did I say "was," I still am). In my teens I experienced the same body issues most teenage girls do. I became obsessed about my weight and the way my body looked. I tried every diet around and believed the hype about the latest and greatest diet pills, drinks, and fizzy tablets to put in your water to curb your appetite – if celebrities were doing it, it was on a TV commercial or in a magazine it must work, right? I worked out excessively, even wrapped myself in plastic wrap while doing cardio to sweat out as many calories as possible. As I grew older and continued on the diet roller coaster, my thirst for knowledge led me to research health and nutrition. All of the generations of women in my family have struggled with their weight so I was genetically on the same path if I didn't break the cycle and find a better solution to maintain a healthy weight for the long term.

Joe and I met in our 20's through a mutual friend at the gym, started out as buddies, grew to love and care for each other and eventually got married. Our diet and exercise similarities grew as we grew together. We learned through research, trial and error what works, what doesn't, and what we need to do to maintain a healthy body, mind and spirit for the rest of our lives. We are both in our late 40's and are in the best shape of our lives, both mentally and physically, by following the plan we are about to share with you.

We both work full-time but make time every day to exercise and eat healthfully. Yes, there are days we splurge, and you should too! But you'll learn to give and take, splurge and work out a little harder to compensate.

We take time on Sunday's to cook, laugh, share time together and prepare our meals for the upcoming week. We enjoy our time in the kitchen and actually use it as a way to decompress. So put on some music, get the family involved and enjoy *your* time together, too.

You hold in your hands the key to a happy, healthy, loving future. We are honored to be able to give you this gift. We wish you all the peace, love, health and happiness you deserve on your journey of life.

~ Heather and Joe

HOW TO USE THIS BOOK

If you already have a way of eating that works for you and you're just looking for some new healthy recipes, feel free to skip this chapter and jump straight to the recipe section.

However, if you feel you need a little more guidance, please continue to read this chapter. You may choose to implement a few of these suggestions or all of them. If you listen to your body, you'll know what's right for you. Trial and error is the only way to know, so pay attention to how you feel each time you eat and modify your cooking and eating habits accordingly.

In order to make educated choices for life, you'll need to know what you're eating and why. Here's a quick breakdown of the basic building blocks of food:

WHAT IS A PROTEIN? Protein is required by the body for growth, maintenance and repair of cells. Proteins are made up of long chain amino acids, which our body requires to function correctly. The amino acids are broken down into:

> **Essential amino acids** which the body cannot produce; they must come from the food we eat.

> **Non-essential amino acids** which are manufactured by the body.

A complete protein is one that contains all of the essential amino acids, like meat, fish, poultry, shellfish, dairy and eggs (we use a lot of egg whites in our cooking as they are the cleanest protein source and contain the highest amount of essential amino acids).

WHAT IS A CARBOHYDRATE? Carbohydrates provide the body fuel and energy and are important to our brain, heart, digestive, nervous and immune systems. Our bodies need a constant supply of energy to function properly.

Simple carbohydrates, also known as sugar, are single sugar molecules or two sugar molecules joined together, foods like sugar and fruits. These foods are broken down quickly in the body.

Complex carbohydrates, or starches, have many sugar molecules and are found in foods like grains, potatoes, brown rice, breads, legumes and vegetables. These are broken down at a slower pace for sustained energy.

WHAT IS A FAT? There are four types of fat:

Saturated and Trans fats, the bad fats, like butter, shortening, fried foods   and processed foods. Stay away from these fats on a daily basis.

Polyunsaturated and Monounsaturated fats, the good fats, like olive oil, nuts, seeds, oily fish and avocados. These fats help keep our cholesterol in check and clean out the arteries to reduce the risk of heart disease. They also help keep us satiated longer, so choose these types of fats on a daily basis.

THE PLAN: HOW TO EAT FOR LIFE

Let me start by saying **THIS IS NOT A DIET BOOK**, it's a plan for you to use and modify to make your own, so cooking, eating and maintaining your weight become as natural as brushing your teeth.

Your body has no need for processed foods, refined sugars or sodas, so steer clear of them in your day-to-day eating. Not only will you *feel* better without these foods in your diet but you'll *look* better, too! And remember that everything you put in your mouth will effect your body, mind and spirit. Be mindful of the cream in your coffee, the sauces and dips on your meals and the glass of wine after work, as they all add up!

Portion control is the key to maintaining your weight so once you find what works, stick with it! Keep in mind that men and very active individuals will need more food to maintain, so pay attention to your body, stop eating *before* you are full and you will learn the proper portion for *you*.

Our recipes are general guidelines of a proper portion so you may want to start there and modify more food or less food once you see how you feel and how your body responds to those specific portions. Each recipe will specify how many servings it makes; we suggest that if you are cooking for one and the recipe makes 2 servings, go ahead and make 2 servings so you have an option already prepared for the next day. In most recipes we'll give you "Make it your own" options so you can learn how to customize foods on your own.

Some people find it helpful to weigh their food until they get used to what a portion looks like. We recommend you get yourself a food scale to take the guesswork out of it so you know you aren't overeating or undereating.

You'll also want to measure your food so, if you don't already have measuring cups and measuring spoons, go out and get some. We have a handy measuring shot glass that measures ounces, teaspoons and tablespoons that we use everyday! In all the recipes in this book, Tbsp. means Tablespoon and tsp. means teaspoon. This is measured with an actual "measuring spoon," not a spoon you eat with.

Every meal should have a balance of proteins, carbohydrates and fats. Be sure to weigh and measure your foods until you get used to that portion size. Try not to eat the same option everyday, switch it up so you experience everything; however, if you find an option that works well for you, eat it as often as you want until your body wants something else. Most meals should consist of *approximately*:

Protein:

Fish, red meats, poultry: women, 4 to 6 ounces; men, 6 to 8 ounces (protein per ounce will vary depending on food source)

Egg whites: 3.6 grams per egg white; we usually have 6 each per meal.

Protein powder: Be sure to get a good quality protein powder with low sugar and follow package for serving size.

Carbohydrates:

Starchy carbs- grains, potatoes and legumes: women, ¼ to ½ cup; men, ½ to 1 cup

Vegetables: start with 2 cups raw or 1 cup cooked and modify accordingly

Fruits: 1 piece (apple, pear, banana, etc.) or ½ to 1 cup (berries, grapes, etc.)

Fats:

Healthy fats like oils, nuts, nut butters, avocados: 1 serving (1 Tbsp. oil, ¼ cup nuts, ¼ avocado)

If you feel like your body doesn't do well with starchy carbs at every meal, feel free to leave them out; you may choose to load up on veggies instead. We realize you won't have all options in every meal, just strive for balance in most meals.

Ideally you should be eating every 3 to 4 hours which means you will eat 5 to 6 times a day. Don't be afraid to eat this often, your body needs the fuel to maintain proper balance. Ladies, you're probably thinking, "I don't even eat breakfast or eat my first meal until noon! I'll gain weight!" Let me tell you, that's exactly why you are stuck and picked up this book in the first place! Your first meal of the day is the time when you wake up your metabolism—when you tell your body "start burning calories now!" If you wait until noon to eat, look at all the hours and calories burned you are missing out on! I am in my late 40's, 5'8" tall and weigh 120 pounds and I religiously eat 6 times a day! This is exactly the plan I follow *every day!* I was not born with a fast metabolism, I created it by eating this way and you can, too.

We recommend you look through the recipes and set a game plan at the beginning of the week so you know what to shop for and to get familiar with the recipes you'll be making. If you have meat or fish in the freezer, take it out in the morning and stick it in the fridge so it's ready to cook at dinner time.

OK… LET'S DO IT!

Pick one "Breakfast" option for your first meal of the day. **Between meals and as your last meal, pick a "Snack, Shake or Dessert" option.** Feel free to make a shake for breakfast instead of a "Breakfast" option If you're short on time; just blend it up and drink it while you're getting ready to go.

Pick one "Lunch" option for lunch. You may choose a dinner option for lunch and vice versa. Any of the "Entrée Salads" are easy lunch options, as are the "One-Plate-Wonders." And be sure to use your leftovers for lunch!

Pick one "Dinner" option for dinner. We've suggested "Side" dishes for each "Main Meal Protein" to make it easy for you to put meals together, but please mix and match however you choose!

We also included a section called "Healthy Entertaining and Indulgences" because, let's face it—ya' gotta live! You're going to have friends and family over and you'll need to be a good host and have some appetizers or munchies for your guests. We'll show you how to entertain and still eat healthfully. This is NOT an option for your day-to-day eating, only occasionally. And we realize you will go *completely* off track on occasion, which is OK too; just make sure you are eating correctly 85 - 90% of the time and be sure to compensate for those extra calories.

We also included "dessert" options in this section to make for your guests. And we know sometimes you just *have* to have dessert and a "Snack, Shake, Dessert" option isn't going to cut it! Choose an option here without getting too far off track, just be sure to compensate somewhere to burn those extra calories and do this only occasionally, not every day.

Make sure you are drinking plenty of water every day to keep your system running smoothly. On average, you should consume ½ ounce water to every pound of body weight daily (Ex: a 120-pound woman should drink minimum 60 ounces of water daily). If you are active, you should be drinking even more. If you're not fond of plain water, add sliced lemon, lime, cucumbers and/or mint—we call it "spa water;" just stay away from sugary fruit juices. Yes, you'll make frequent trips to the rest room, but think of the extra calories you'll burn while you're getting up and down all day, as well as flushing out the fat and toxins to keep you healthy!

To be healthy *and* fit, you will need to exercise. Try to achieve a balance of cardiovascular exercises and weight bearing exercises. There are plenty of different exercise programs out there, so find one you like so you'll stick with it. We like High Intensity Interval Training (HIIT) because we can get our cardio and weights done in about 20 to 40 minutes total—great for the days when we're pressed for time.

Remember: Life's a journey, not a diet...
let the journey begin!

ITEMS TO ALWAYS HAVE IN
YOUR KITCHEN

This is a cheat-sheet of items we like to keep stocked at our house. Choose organic when possible and low sodium options if available. Most stores have pre-packaged veggies, lettuce, fruits and grains that are ready to eat, which makes it really convenient when you don't have a lot of time to prepare a meal.

We have found that eating foods with gluten bloat us and make us sluggish so we prefer to eat gluten-free. If you don't experience any issues with gluten, feel free to eat these foods.

FOR THE PANTRY
Grains:

    rice (we like brown rice)

    quinoa

    couscous*

    pasta*

    barley*

Cereals: (no sugar added)

    oats

    buckwheat

    cream of rice

    cream of wheat*

Oils:

olive oil (for cooking)

extra virgin olive oil (for dressings, dips)

sesame oil

coconut oil

Vinegars:

red wine vinegar

Balsamic vinegar

apple cider vinegar

Spices:

cinnamon

basil

oregano

thyme

rosemary

garlic powder (not garlic *salt*)

cumin

turmeric

cayenne pepper

red chili flakes/ crushed red pepper

paprika or smoked paprika

sea salt

black pepper

Sweeteners:

honey

agave

coconut nectar

Xylitol or stevia

pure maple syrup

Drinks:

almond milk (unsweetened)

coconut milk (unsweetened)

coffee

tea (unsweetened)

club soda

Legumes: (canned is OK, just rinse and drain first)

black beans

red beans

garbanzo/chick peas

lentils

Extras:

protein powder of choice (keep the sodium and sugar low)

protein bars (same as above)

canned tomatoes (no salt added)

canned tuna or salmon (packed in water, no salt added)

almond meal or bread crumbs*

chicken, beef or vegetable stock

cocoa powder (unsweetened)

vanilla extract

FOR THE FREEZER

Berries (variety)

Vegetables (variety)

Meats:

> chicken breast
>
> ground beef
>
> ground turkey
>
> pork tenderloin

Fish:

> salmon
>
> tilapia
>
> halibut
>
> mahi mahi
>
> your favorite fish of choice

FOR THE FRIDGE

Fruits: (choose a wide variety including):

> apples
>
> bananas
>
> berries
>
> lemons
>
> limes
>
> avocados

Vegetables: (choose a wide variety including):

> spinach
>
> kale

mixed greens

bell peppers (all colors)

broccoli

beets

cauliflower

asparagus

zucchini

onions

garlic

potatoes

sweet potatoes

Extras:

flax seed/meal

mustard

salsa

jarred sundried tomatoes

jarred olives

hot sauces

low-sodium soy sauce, tamari or coconut aminos

nuts (variety, unsalted; especially almonds, cashews and walnuts)

nut butters (variety, all natural, no sugar or sweetener added)

eggs

bread* (Ezekiel/Food for Life makes healthy bread; gluten-free bread, too)

TIPS AND TRICKS

Through the years, we've developed some tips and tricks that make our lives a little easier and we want to share them with you!

Follow the plan 85 - 90% of the time but allow yourself the occasional indulgence- you deserve it! When you do indulge, limit yourself to a few bites of the forbidden food, not the whole thing! And make sure to get right back on track at your next meal.

Take some time on Sunday to prepare part of your meals for the week. Do some prep work to make your life a little easier during the busy week. Freeze any prepared dishes you will be eating later in the week.

Even if you are cooking for one, go ahead and make extra so you have some for the next day. And when you make some rice or quinoa, make a big batch to use it throughout the week. They even freeze well, so you know you are always prepared.

3,500 calories = 1 pound. If you need to lose a few pounds, you'll need to consume fewer calories and/or burn off extra calories through exercise.

Choose organic whenever possible. If fruit or vegetables have a product code sticker on them and it's 4-digit number- it was grown with pesticides; if it's a 5-digit number beginning with a "9"- it's organic and not genetically modified; if it's a 5-digit number beginning with an "8"- it's been genetically modified so don't buy it! We realize buying organic is more expensive, so you may choose to only buy organic where it matters most. Go to the Environmental Working Group's website at www.EWG.org/foodnews for a list of items you should always buy organic (they also have a handy app for your phone called Dirty Dozen).

Save your more expensive extra virgin olive oil for dips and dressings, as it has a lower smoking point (the cooking temperature that the oil starts to break down and release toxins). Use virgin olive oil (not refined) for cooking as it has a higher smoke point; or use coconut oil (unrefined or virgin), which has a higher smoking point as well.

Peel and Freeze bananas for a creamier protein drink or smoothie.

Get a standard ice cube tray. Freeze chicken or vegetable stock so you always have it on hand as well as almond milk or coconut milk for smoothies. Measure how much fits in one cube— mine are 1 ounce so I always know how much I'm using in my recipes and smoothies. I like to freeze my already-opened containers of stock, almond milk and coconut milk that are approaching the expiration date – no wasting food in our household!

Fill up a large water bottle or pitcher in the morning and make sure you drink it all by the end of the day–it's a good way to see that you are meeting your water quota. (We use a 64-ounce BPA-free refillable plastic bottle everyday, sold at www.Bluewave.com.)

Keep scotch tape and a sharpie in your kitchen to label your leftovers so you never end up throwing away food that's gone bad. I just write the date prepared on a piece of tape and stick it to my container before putting it in the fridge, and I always write the date opened on items in jars and cartons.

Get a measure shot glass that measures tablespoons, teaspoons and ounces. This is my savior when it comes to measuring small amounts of liquid so I know exactly what I'm putting in my food. I measure my coffee creamer with it in the morning, too.

Having an organized kitchen makes for a much happier and efficient time cooking. Make sure your most-used spices and pantry items are easily accessible; clean out the pots and pans cupboard and show them the respect they deserve–you will be using them daily, so be sure they're handy; and put your most-used utensils in a holder on the counter.

Find your favorite jeans that make you feel and look great and make a habit of putting them on every couple of weeks to make sure they still look amazing on you. If they are a little snug, it's time to modify your eating and/or workouts.

Develop traditions in your household with your meals so you have something specific to look forward to. In our home, it's "Burger Friday" and "Pasta Sunday".

RECIPES

BREAKFAST

Not your Mama's Oatmeal

Makes 1 serving

~ ¼ cup quick cook steel cut oats or ½ cup rolled oats
(check package for serving size)

~ ¾ cups water

~ 6 egg whites

~ dash of cinnamon

~ ¼ cup walnuts, or your favorite nuts

~ drizzle of honey

Put the water, oats and cinnamon in a sauce pan and cover, cook on medium heat until it boils then turn it on low and stir occasionally until the water is absorbed. (Watch 'em—you don't know how many times I've made a mess of the stove when it boils over!) Meanwhile, put egg whites in a saute pan with some cooking spray, and stir as they cook until they're white and no longer runny; put eggs and oats in a bowl and top with nuts and a drizzle of honey.

Make it your own:
- ✓ Substitute 1 Tbsp. of your favorite nut butter for the egg whites; you won't get as much protein but it's nice to switch it up once in a while
- ✓ Need more fiber? Add 1 to 2 Tbsp. flax or chia seeds

- ✓ Use cream of rice, cream of wheat, cream of buckwheat or buckwheat groats instead of the oats
- ✓ Mix in ½ cup berries for antioxidants
- ✓ Top with 2 Tbsp. almond milk or coconut milk

Smokey Salmon and The Miracles

Makes 1 serving

~ 2 slices bread

~ 2 slices beefsteak tomato

~ 1 slice red onion

~ 1 Tbsp. capers, rinsed in water

~ 2 Tbsp. light cream cheese

~ 2 oz. smoked salmon*

~ 1 whole egg

Crack egg in a pan sprayed with cooking spray being careful not to break the yolk. Flip it when it's semi-set and cook about another 30 to 45 seconds so the yolk is still a little runny- this is called "over easy". Toast your bread to desired doneness and spread with cream cheese; layer remaining ingredients and top with egg.

Make it your own:
✓ Substitute ¼ avocado for the cream cheese and take out toppers that you don't like

* *Make sure salmon has no nitrites or sodium benzoate and look for option with lowest grams sodium.*

Spanish Spinach Omelet

Makes 1 serving

~ 6 egg whites

~ 1 cup spinach

~ 2 Tbsp. salsa

~ ¼ avocado

~ ½ tsp. oregano or spice of choice

~ black pepper to taste

Put egg whites and seasoning in a pan sprayed with cooking spray and cook until set enough to flip; flip eggs, top with spinach and cover with a lid to steam the spinach; fold omelet in half, put it on a plate and top with salsa and avocado. If your eggs don't flip and you make a mess of it just turn it into a scramble instead!

Make it your own:
- ✓ Add ¼ cup diced peppers
- ✓ Substitute ¼ cup of your favorite veggies instead of spinach
- ✓ If you like it spicy, top with hot sauce or salsa
- ✓ If you need more carbs, have a slice of toast with it or make a breakfast burrito by wrapping it in a large low-cal wrap or tortilla

Haulin' Oats- Baked Oatmeal To-Go

Makes 12; 1 serving = 1 to 2 muffins

~ 1 egg

~ ½ tsp. vanilla extract

~ 1 cup unsweetened applesauce

~ ½ ripe banana, mashed

~ ¼ cup honey

~ 2 ½ cups oats

~ 2 Tbsp. flax seed or flax meal

~ 1 ½ tsp. baking powder

~ 2 tsp. cinnamon

~ ½ tsp. sea salt

~ 1 ½ cups almond milk

Add-in's (optional): shredded coconut, nuts, fresh fruit, dried fruit, chocolate chips

Pre-heat oven to 350 degrees; mix egg, vanilla, applesauce, banana and honey to combine; add oats, flax, baking powder, salt and cinnamon and stir to combine; pour in milk and mix well; stir in add-in's; pour into muffin tins sprayed with cooking spray and bake 30 minutes or until toothpick inserted comes out clean. Store in fridge or freezer; reheat when ready to eat or eat 'em cold.

Yogi Berry Bowl

Makes 1 serving

~ 1 cup plain, non-fat or low-fat Greek yogurt

~ ¼ cup nuts of choice

~ ½ cup berries of choice

~ drizzle of honey or agave

Put all ingredients in a bowl and enjoy!

Make it your own:

✓ If you need more fiber, add 1 to 2 Tbsp. flax or chia seeds

✓ If you need more protein, add ½ serving protein powder or 1 Tbsp. nut butter

✓ Substitute fruit of choice instead of berries – peaches or bananas would be great too!

Cinnamon French Toast with Eggs

Makes 1 serving

~ 5 egg whites

~ 2 Tbsp. almond or coconut milk

~ 1 tsp. vanilla extract

~ ½ tsp. cinnamon

~ 1 tsp. coconut oil

~ 2 slices bread

Mix eggs, milk, vanilla and cinnamon in a pie tin or deep plate and dip bread, covering both sides in egg; cook in pan or griddle coated with coconut oil, flipping when each side is browned; cook remaining eggs in pan stirring to scramble, until cooked through, then serve.

Make it your own:
- ✓ For more fiber, sprinkle with flax or chia seeds
- ✓ Top with Greek yogurt, berries, sliced apple or banana

Quinoa Pancakes

Makes 6 medium pancakes; 2 to 3 pancakes is a serving

~ 2/3 cup cooked quinoa (red or white, cooked with water according to package)

~ 2/3 cup flour

~ 1 ½ Tbsp. pure maple syrup, agave, honey or coconut nectar

~ ½ tsp. cinnamon

~ 1 tsp. baking powder

~ ¼ tsp. of salt

~ ½ cup almond milk (or coconut milk)*

~ 1 whole egg

~ ½ tsp. vanilla extract

~ ¼ tsp. coconut oil, melted

Combine flour, sugar, cinnamon, baking powder and salt in a bowl; in another bowl combine milk, eggs, vanilla and coconut oil, then add it to dry ingredients; fold in quinoa until well blended. Using a 1/3 cup measuring cup pour onto a hot griddle or pan coated with cooking spray; cook until top is covered with bubbles, then flip, cooking until golden.

Make the batter the night before for a fluffier pancake, just increase the milk from ½ cup to ¾ cup.

Make it your own:
✓ Top with Greek yogurt and bananas or berries, and/or maple

syrup

✓ You can make these gluten free by using gluten-free flour or almond flour instead of regular flour

SNACKS, SHAKES AND DESSERTS

You may have anything in this section for your between-meal snacks or dessert on a daily basis; mix it up for variety. We like to use plain or vanilla protein powder so we can modify the flavor by the other ingredients we add, but feel free to use what you have. And if you need more fiber in any of your shakes, go ahead and add 1 Tbsp. flax or chia seeds. For dessert we like to use more ice and less liquid in our shakes so we get an ice cream consistency and we eat it with a spoon—you can make any of the shakes as "ice cream" this way.

Green Machine
Makes 1 serving

~ 1 cup almond milk or coconut milk

~ 1 cup kale and/or spinach

~ ½ to 1 apple or pear, diced

~ 1 serving protein powder

~ ice

Mix all in a blender and drink.

Make it your own:
✓ Add 1 stalk celery, handful parsley, grated fresh ginger and/or ½ cucumber

Very Berry Smoothie

Makes 1 serving

~ 1 cup almond milk or coconut milk

~ 1 cup frozen berries of choice

~ 1 serving protein powder

~ ice

Mix all in a blender and drink.

> **Make it your own:**
> ✓ Add 1 Tbsp. unsweetened cocoa powder for a chocolate-berry smoothie

Go Bananas Shake

Makes 1 serving

~ 1 cup almond milk or coconut milk

~ 1 frozen banana

~ 1 serving protein powder

~ ice

Mix all in a blender and drink.

> **Make it your own:**
> ✓ Add 1 Tbsp. unsweetened cocoa powder for a chocolate banana shake
> ✓ Add 1 Tbsp. nut butter, nuts or almond meal for a banana-nut shake
> ✓ Add 3 or 4 dates for a banana date shake

Who put Chocolate in my Peanut Butter Shake

Makes 1 serving

~ 1 cup almond milk or coconut milk

~ 1 Tbsp. nut butter

~ 1 Tbsp. cocoa powder

~ 1 serving protein powder

~ ice

Mix all in a blender and drink.

> **Make it your own:**
> ✓ For a dessert "ice cream" option, make it thick and top with a few slices banana for banana split!
> ✓ Make a nut butter mocha by using 1 cup of cold coffee instead of almond/coconut milk

---

PB & J Shake

Makes 1 serving

~ 1 cup almond milk or coconut milk

~ 1 Tbsp. nut butter

~ ½ to 1 cup frozen berries

~ 1 serving protein powder

~ ice

Mix all in a blender and drink.

> **Make it your own:**
> ✓ Use 1 apple or pear instead of berries

Mint Chocolate Chip Ice Cream

Makes 1 serving

~ 4 almond milk or coconut milk ice cubes (½ cup)

~ ¼ cup almond milk or coconut milk

~ ½ ounce dark chocolate bar

~ 3 to 4 fresh mint leaves

~ 1 serving protein powder

Mix all in a blender and drink. Add a little more almond milk, coconut milk or water if it's too thick to blend.

> **Make it your own:**
> ✓ Not a fan of mint? Leave it out.
> ✓ Make chocolate chocolate chip ice cream by adding 1 Tbsp. cocoa powder

Sour Head Protein Balls

Makes 2 servings

~ ¼ cup protein powder

~ ¼ cup almonds

~ 1 Tbsp. honey

~ 1 Tbsp. lemon juice

Mix all together in a food processor to form a stiff dough; add a few drops of water if it's too dry and not sticking together; divide into fourths and roll into balls. Store them in the fridge to keep them firm. These are great to make ahead of time and take with you as a snack.

Make it your own:
- ✓ For chocolate balls, use water instead of lemon juice and add 1 Tbsp. cocoa powder
- ✓ Add 1 tsp. flavored extract for virtually any flavor: we've used anise (tastes like black licorice), cherry, rum… you name it, the possibilities are endless.

Snap, Apple Crisp

Makes 1 serving

~ 1 apple, cored and diced

~ ½ tsp. cinnamon

~ 2 Tbsp. almond meal or finely chopped nuts

~ 2 tsp. honey, agave, coconut nectar, or 1 packet sweetener

~ 1 tsp. coconut oil

Put apple in microwave-safe bowl with a few spoonfuls of water and toss with cinnamon. Microwave for about 2 minutes until apple is soft (you could do this in a pan on the stove instead if you wanted); mix almond meal or nuts, sweetener and coconut oil and put on top of apple; put under the oven broiler for about a minute or until topping is golden brown. This would be great with some Greek yogurt on top, too!

Make it your own:
✓ Pear, peach or any kind of berries (fresh or frozen) would work, too!

But Wait, There's More! There's lots of options that require little to no prep, such as:

- 1 Apple with 2 Tbsp. nut butter or ¼ cup nuts
- Celery stalks with 2 Tbsp. nut butter or ¼ cup nuts
- 1 cup Greek yogurt with cinnamon, ½ cup berries and drizzle of honey
- ¼ to ½ cup **Hummus*** with veggies (celery, carrots, cucumber, tomatoes)
- ½ to 1 cup **Cucumber Yogurt dip*** with veggies
- Protein bar

* See Dressings, Dips and Sauces section for recipes

EASY LUNCHES

Joey's Tuna Salad with Apples and Walnuts

Makes 1 to 2 servings

~ 1 can chunk light tuna in water

~ ¼ cup Greek yogurt

~ 1 tsp. dill spice

~ ½ apple, diced

~ 2 Tbsp. walnuts, chopped

~ ¼ tsp. sea salt

~ ½ tsp. black pepper

Rinse and drain tuna; mix all ingredients together until combined and serve over lettuce, rice or quinoa.

Make it your own:
- ✓ Cinnamon would be a great substitute for the dill for a sweet option, just leave out the pepper
- ✓ Use any kind of nuts or substitute sunflower seeds; if you need more fiber add some flax, too!
- ✓ Keep your tuna salad and lettuce separate until you're ready to eat so the lettuce doesn't get soggy

Chickity Chinese "Fried" Quinoa

Makes 1 to 2 servings

~ 2 tsp. olive oil

~ ¼ cup carrots, diced

~ ¼ cup peas (frozen is OK)

~ ¼ cup prepared quinoa

~ 1 Tbsp. leeks or onions, diced

~ 6 eggs, whites only

~ 2 tsp. soy sauce (or Tamari or coconut aminos)

Put all ingredients except eggs in a pan with olive oil and cook on medium heat until heated through; add egg whites and continue cooking until eggs are cooked; add soy sauce, stir to combine and serve.

Jamaican-Me-Hungry Bean and Rice Muffins

Makes 9; 1 serving = 1 to 2 muffins

~ 1 ½ cups prepared brown rice

~ 1 ¼ cups canned black lentils, rinsed and drained

~ ¼ cup jalapenos, diced (jarred or fresh)

~ ¼ cup leeks or onions, finely diced

~ (1) 15 ½ ounce can red beans, rinsed, drained and mashed

~ ¾ cups coconut milk, unsweetened

~ 2 cups chopped fresh spinach

~ 2 whole eggs

~ 2 tsp. garlic powder

~ 2 tsp. thyme

~ ½ tsp. sea salt

~ 1 tsp. black pepper

Preheat oven to 350 degrees; mix all ingredients together in a bowl until well combined; spoon into muffin tins lined with muffin liners (or spray with cooking spray if you don't have liners- they may not stay together as well, though); divide between 9 muffins; bake 55 to 60 minutes; store in fridge or freezer. Heat before eating or eat 'em cold!

You Just Want More! There are plenty of other easy, healthy lunch options such as:

- **Entrée Salads** or **Build-Your-Own Salads** make great to-go lunches, just keep your dressing separate until you're ready to eat or you'll end up with a soggy mess
- **One-Plate Wonders** are easy to-go options
- Get creative with your leftover's. Mix and match any proteins, salads and sides to create something new- you just might make a favorite creation this way!

DRESSINGS, DIPS AND SAUCES

Colonel Mustard Dressing

Makes about 1 cup

~ ½ cup plain Greek yogurt

~ 1 Tbsp. Dijon mustard

~ 1 Tbsp. yellow mustard

~ ½ Tbsp. honey

~ 1 Tbsp. white wine vinegar

Mix all together and serve. Don't have white wine vinegar? Use red wine vinegar or apple cider vinegar instead.

Hail Caesar Dressing

Makes about 1 cup

~ 1 clove garlic, minced (chopped up really small)

~ 3 Tbsp. lemon juice

~ 2 Tbsp. plain Greek yogurt

~ 2 tsp. Dijon mustard

~ 3 Tbsp. grated parmesan cheese

~ 3 Tbsp. extra virgin olive oil

Mix all together and serve.

Make a simple Caesar Salad with chopped Romaine lettuce, cherry tomatoes cut in half, a Tbsp. of sunflower seeds and a sprinkle of parmesan cheese.

Ranch-style Dressing

Makes about 1 cup

~ 1 cup plain Greek yogurt

~ 2 Tbsp. grated red onion

~ 2 Tbsp. chopped parsley

~ 1 Tbsp. fresh dill (or ½ tsp. dried dill)

~ 1 Tbsp. lemon juice

~ 1 tsp. extra virgin olive oil

~ 1 clove garlic, minced (chopped up really small)

~ ½ tsp. sea salt

~ 1 tsp. black pepper

Mix all together and serve. Don't like onion? Don't use it or substitute 1 tsp. garlic powder instead.

Yo' Adrian Italian Dressing

Makes about 1 cup

~ 2 Tbsp. red wine vinegar

~ 2 Tbsp. fresh lemon juice

~ 1 Tbsp. Dijon mustard

~ ¼ cup extra virgin olive oil

~ 1 clove garlic, minced (chopped up really small)

~ ¼ tsp. each dried oregano, basil, thyme, rosemary (or 1 tsp. Italian seasoning)

~ ¼ tsp. sea salt

~ ½ tsp. black pepper

Mix all together and serve.

Dijon Vinaigrette

Makes about 1 cup

~ ¼ cup Dijon mustard

~ ¼ cup yellow mustard

~ ¼ cup extra virgin olive oil

~ ¼ cup red wine vinegar

~ 1 tsp. sea salt

~ 1 tsp. black pepper

Mix all together and serve.

Tasty Taco Topper, the Triple 'T'

Makes about 2 servings

~ ½ cup plain Greek yogurt

~ 1 Tbsp. lime juice

~ ½ tsp. extra virgin olive oil

~ ¼ tsp. paprika or smoked paprika

Mix all together and serve on tacos, burritos, salads or eggs. If you like a thinner sauce, add a little water to it.

Da Bomb BBQ Sauce

Makes about 1 cup

~ 2 Tbsp. olive oil

~ ½ onion, diced

~ 2 Tbsp. tomato paste

~ 1 Tbsp. red wine vinegar

~ 2 Tbsp. molasses

~ 1 Tbsp. yellow mustard

~ 1 Tbsp. Dijon mustard

~ 2 Tbsp. Worcestershire

~ ½ cup water

Sautee onion in olive oil until translucent, about 3 to 4 minutes; Add remaining ingredients, bring to a boil, then simmer on low for 10 to 15 minutes. Let cool, then pour through a strainer and discard the onions. Store in the fridge.

If you like it spicy go ahead and add a little chili sauce or chili powder!

Cucumber Yogurt Dip

Makes about 2 cups; 1 serving is ½ to 1 cup

~ 2 cups plain Greek yogurt

~ 2 cucumbers peeled, seeded and diced

~ 2 Tbsp. extra virgin olive oil

~ 1 Tbsp. lemon juice

~ 2 cloves garlic, minced (chopped up really small)

~ ½ tsp. sea salt

~ ½ tsp. black pepper

Mix all together and chill before serving. Great with veggies or with **Mediterranean Chicken** (see *Main Protein* for recipe).

Make it your own:
✓ Change it up by adding 1 Tbsp. dried mint.

Hummus Among Us

Makes about 2 cups; 1 serving is ½ to 1 cup

~ 1 can garbanzo beans, drained and rinsed

~ ¼ cup tahini (in ethnic food aisle at grocery store)

~ ¼ cup lemon juice

~ 2 cloves garlic, minced (chopped up really small)

~ 2 Tbsp. extra virgin olive oil

~ 1 tsp. sea salt

~ dash of paprika to sprinkle on top before serving

Mix all together in a food processor; store in refrigerator. Use as a dip for veggies like carrots or celery or make some Brown Rice Tortilla Chips, see below.

Make it your own:

✓ Don't have tahini? Leave it out and now it's bean dip!

✓ **Make your own tortilla chips:** slice a brown rice tortilla or corn tortilla like a pizza so you have triangles; sprinkle with sea salt, then crisp them in a pan with a little cooking spray.

SIDES

STARCHY CARBS

Simple Saffron Rice

Makes 2 to 4 servings

~ ½ cup Jasmine or basmati rice

~ 1 cup low-sodium chicken stock or water

~ ¼ tsp. turmeric

~ ¼ tsp. saffron*

Bring the chicken stock or water to a boil in a small pan with lid; then add seasonings, stirring to combine; add rice, turn to low heat and put lid on to simmer for about 15 minutes or until all liquid is absorbed; fluff with a fork and serve.

* Saffron comes in little "threads" and are very flavorful, you will only need a few threads, about ¼ tsp.

Make it your own:
- ✓ If you have a rice cooker, use it!
- ✓ For a really quick version, use prepared brown rice packets or any leftover plain rice; add a little water and seasonings above; heat on low until all liquid is absorbed.

South of the Border Spanish Rice

Makes 2 to 4 servings

~ ½ cup medium or long grain white rice

~ 2 tsp. olive oil

~ ½ clove garlic, minced (chopped up really small)

~ 2 slices onion, minced

~ 1 cup low-sodium chicken or vegetable broth

~ 2 tsp. tomato paste

~ ¼ tsp. each oregano, sea salt, black pepper

In a large pan, brown the rice in olive oil over medium to high heat. Add the onion and garlic and cook until softened, about 4 minutes. Add the remaining ingredients and bring to a boil; then simmer on low until all the liquid is absorbed, about 15 to 20 minutes.

Make it your own:
- ✓ Add hot sauce or chili powder if you like it spicy
- ✓ Use brown rice for a healthier version
- ✓ For a really quick version, just add ¼ cup of your favorite salsa to prepared rice and heat until salsa is absorbed.

Oh-So-Sweet Potato Fries

Makes 1 to 2 servings

~ 1 large sweet potato

~ 1 Tbsp. olive oil

~ 1 tsp. sea salt

~ 1 tsp. cinnamon (optional)

Scrub and dry potato, cut in half lengthwise then in half lengthwise again and again until you have fries in your desired size. Toss fries in a bowl with olive oil, salt and cinnamon then cook in a pan or on a flat BBQ griddle until browned on the outside and soft inside, about 15 minutes.

> **Make it your own:**
> ✓ Use a russet/baking potato instead and leave out the cinnamon for traditional fries.

Potato Hash

Makes 1 to 2 servings

~ 1 large potato, finely diced

~ 2 Tbsp. onion, finely diced

~ 1 Tbsp. olive oil

~ 1 tsp. sea salt

Put all ingredients in a pan and cook over medium to high heat until browned.

Make it your own:

✓ Don't like onion? Leave it out.

✓ Add 2 Tbsp. finely diced bell peppers for more flavor

✓ Add chili powder or smoked paprika for some heat!

Keen on Quinoa

Makes 2 to 4 servings

~ ½ cup quinoa (red or white)

~ 1 cup low-sodium chicken or vegetable broth

~ ¼ tsp. sea salt

~ ½ tsp. black pepper

~ ¼ cup fresh cilantro or parsley, chopped

Rinse quinoa in water and drain it; bring broth to a boil and add quinoa, salt and pepper and bring to a boil again; cover and simmer on low until liquid is absorbed, about 15 minutes. Add cilantro or parsley, fluff with a fork and serve.

Make it your own:
✓ Make plain quinoa by substituting water for the broth and leave out the seasonings. This is great to have on hand and season as you use it, or use it plain for **Quinoa Pancakes!** (see Breakfast for recipe).

SIDES

VEGGIES

Side Salad 101

Makes 2 servings

~ 2 cups mixed greens

~ 1 tomato

~ 1 cucumber

~ 1 tsp. sunflower seeds (seeded, no shell)

~ Dressing of choice (see *Dressings, Dips and Sauces*)

Slice or dice tomato and cucumber and put on top of greens with sunflower seeds and dressing of choice.

Make it your own:

✓ Use spinach or any other favorite salad greens; most stores have pre-packaged varieties that are ready to eat

✓ Add or substitute veggies as you wish

Krazy Kale Salad

Makes 2 servings

~ 2 - 3 cups Tuscan kale

~ 1 Tbsp. lemon juice

~ 1 Tbsp. olive oil

~ 1 clove garlic, minced

~ 2 Tbsp. almond meal (or finely grind almonds in a food
processor)

~ ¼ tsp. each sea salt, black pepper, red chili flakes

Remove the ribs from the kale (the hard middle part) and chop into bite-size pieces (some stores have kale sliced and packaged); Toss with remaining ingredients and serve.

Make it your own:
- ✓ Substitute ground sunflower seeds for the almond meal for a different flavor
- ✓ Add 1 Tbsp. parmesan cheese

Asian Cole Slaw

Makes 2 servings

~ 6 ounces shredded cabbage (most stores have pre-
   shredded packages)

~ 1 tsp. grated ginger

~ 2 Tbsp. lime juice

~ 1 Tbsp. sesame oil

~ ¼ cup fresh cilantro, chopped

~ 1 Tbsp. sesame seeds

~ 1 Tbsp. leek, chopped

~ 1 Tbsp. slivered almonds

~ ¼ tsp. sea salt

~ ½ tsp. black pepper

Mix it all together, that's it- Done! *This would make a great All-In-One meal, just add grilled chicken or fish!*

For a Basic Cole Slaw, *just use extra virgin olive oil instead of sesame oil and leave out the ginger, sesame seeds and almonds.*

Quick Roasted Tomatoes

Makes 2 servings

~ 3 Roma tomatoes

~ ½ Tbsp. olive oil

~ ¼ tsp. sea salt

Slice tomatoes in half lengthwise then slice each half in half again. Coat in olive oil and sprinkle with salt. Cook in pan on high heat until browned on all sides. This is also great to do on the BBQ!

Burnt Brussel Sprouts

Makes 2 servings

~ 1 pound brussel sprouts (Trader Joe's has 'em bagged
    and ready to go, no stalks)

~ 1 Tbsp. olive oil

~ ¼ tsp. sea salt

Cut stem end off brussel sprouts and discard stems. Cut each brussel sprout in half; toss with olive oil and salt, then grill in a pan over medium to high heat tossing occasionally until browned on all sides.

These would be great on the BBQ, too- just put 'em on skewers whole and grill 'em!

Garlic Cauliflower Smash

Makes 2 servings

~ Cauliflower, ½ head or 12 ounce bag florets

~ 1 tsp. olive oil

~ 1 small clove garlic, chopped

~ 1 Tbsp. low-fat cream cheese

~ ¼ tsp. sea salt

Put cauliflower in a deep pan, cover with water and boil until soft and tender, about 10 minutes. Meanwhile, cook garlic in a small pan with olive oil about 2 minutes. Drain water from cauliflower; put cauliflower and remaining ingredients in a blender and blend until smooth and creamy. (If you have an immersion blender, use that instead)

Make it your own:

✓ Add 1 Tbsp. parmesan cheese for parmesan smash

MAIN PROTEINS

Mediterranean Chicken

Makes 2 to 4 servings

~ 1 pound chicken breasts

~ ¼ tsp. saffron, dissolved in 1 Tbsp. hot water

~ 1/3 cup lime juice

~ 1 Tbsp. olive oil

~ 1 clove garlic, minced (chopped up really small)

~ ¼ cup plain Greek yogurt

~ ½ tsp. sea salt

~ 1 tsp. black pepper

Mix all ingredients except chicken until combined; soak chicken in it for at least 10 minutes, or as long as overnight. Cook in a pan coated with 1 Tbsp. olive oil until cooked through.

> **Make it your own:**
> ✓ This is also great to do on the BBQ!
> ✓ Short on time? Cut the chicken into 1 inch cubes and cook in pan- it will cook up faster than a whole breast and it's great over rice!

Suggested side dishes:

- **Simple Saffron Rice** (see *Sides: starchy carbs*). If you're making this as a side, make this first then start your chicken since the rice takes about 20 minutes to cook.

- **Quick Roasted Tomatoes** (see *Sides: Vegetables*). Do this last as it only takes a few minutes.
- **Hummus and/or Cucumber Yogurt Dip** (see *Dressings, Dips and Sauces)*. Make this while your chicken is cooking.
- **Brown Rice Tortilla Chips** (see Hummus recipe in *Dressings, Dips and Sauces)*. Make this while your chicken is cooking.

Un-Fried 'Fried' Chicken

Makes 2 to 4 servings

~ 1 pound chicken breasts

~ ½ cup plain Greek yogurt

~ 1 tsp. hot sauce

~ ¼ cup almond meal

~ ¼ cup crushed potato chips

~ ¼ tsp. each garlic powder, oregano, paprika, sea salt, pepper

~ 1 Tbsp. olive oil

Mix yogurt and hot sauce in a shallow dish; mix almond meal, chips and spices in another dish; dip chicken in the yogurt mix then in almond mix to coat both sides; cook in pan with olive oil over medium heat until browned then turn; cook until cooked through.

Make it your own:
✓ Make parmesan chicken by adding 2 Tbsp. parmesan cheese to the almond meal mixture
✓ Short on time? Cut the chicken into small cubes or strips before coating in almond meal mixture- they'll cook faster (and you can call 'em 'chicken nuggets' if you have kids!)

Suggested side dishes:

• **Garlic Cauliflower Smash** or **Potato Hash** (see *Sides*)

• **Krazy Kale Salad** or **Side Salad 101** (see *Sides:*

Vegetables) or **Green Bean 'Fries'** (see *Burger Friday* in this section for recipe).

Burger Friday!

Makes 2 servings

~ 1 pound lean ground beef or turkey*

~ ½ tsp. each: basil, oregano, thyme, black pepper

~ ¼ tsp. each: garlic, sea salt (or try smoked sea salt),
   paprika (or smoked paprika)

~ toppings of choice like cheese, lettuce, sliced tomato,
   avocado, mustard, fried egg

* This amount of meat is more than you need for this recipe; you can either cook up all 4 burgers or save ½ the raw meat for another time, like for meat sauce with pasta!

Mix all ingredients just until combined (don't overmix it or your finished burger will be tough). Divide meat into fourths and form 4 patties (or 2, if you're only cooking up ½). Cook in pan with a little olive oil or cooking spray until browned on both sides. If you're using cheese, place it on top when your burger is almost done, put a lid on the pan and let the cheese melt. Burgers are also great on the BBQ!

We like to eat our burger without the bun- just squirt a little mustard on your plate, put your burger on it, then toppings. One of our favorite toppings is a fried egg right on top! Sounds strange, but try it- you might love it! And sometimes we use toasted gluten-free bread as a bun.

Suggested side dishes:

- **Oh-So-Sweet Potato Fries** (see *Sides: starchy carbs*)
- **Potato Hash** (see *Sides: starchy carbs*)
- **Green Bean Fries:** toss green beans in a little olive oil, sprinkle with salt and cook 'em up til browned, either in a pan or on a griddle on the BBQ.
- **Side Salad 101** (see *Sides: Vegetables*).

Wasabi Ahi
Makes 2 to 4 servings

~ 1 pound Ahi tuna (Mahi Mahi is good here, too)

~ ¼ cup soy sauce (or tamari or coconut aminos)

~ 1 tsp. wasabi

~ 1 clove garlic, minced

~ 1 Tbsp. olive oil plus another Tbsp. for cooking

~ ¼ tsp. sea salt

~ ½ tsp. black pepper

Mix all ingredients and marinate fish 30 to 60 minutes; cook in pan with olive oil, topping fish with remaining marinade, until browned and cooked through (great on the BBQ, too!).

Make it your own:
- ✓ No wasabi? Try red chili sauce instead (AKA Rooster sauce)
- ✓ Top with sesame seeds before serving

Suggested side dishes:

- **Asian Cole Slaw** or **Burnt Brussel Sprouts** (see *Sides: Vegetables*).

- **Keen on Quinoa** (see *Sides: starchy carbs*) or **Brown Rice** (cook according to package)

The Little Salmon that Could

Makes 2 to 4 servings

~ 2 Tbsp. Kalamata olives, chopped

~ 2 Tbsp. sun dried tomatoes, chopped (jarred in oil)

~ 2 cloves garlic, minced

~ 1 Tbsp. olive oil

~ 2 Tbsp. Dijon mustard

~ 1 tsp. rosemary (fresh, chopped or dried spice)

~ 1 tsp. thyme (fresh, chopped or dried spice)

~ ½ cup almond meal

~ 1 pound salmon filets, no skin

Preheat oven to 400 degrees; mix all ingredients except salmon in a bowl until combined; place salmon on a foil-lined baking sheet sprayed with cooking spray, top with topping mixture and bake for 15 minutes or until opaque in center.

Suggested side dishes:

- **Burnt Brussel Sprouts** and/or **Side Salad 101** (see *Sides* for recipes)
- **Parmesan Cauliflower Smash** (see *Sides: starchy carbs*)

This would also be a great All-In-One meal over any of the side salads!

Pulled Pork Tacos

Makes about 4 servings

~ 1 pound pork tenderloin

~ 2 cups BBQ Sauce (see *Dressings, Dips and Sauces*)

~ 8 corn or flour tortillas

Put pork and BBQ sauce in a slow cooker/crock pot and make sure meat is covered, if not, add a little water; cook on high for 4 hours or low for 8 hours then shred pork with a fork, it should pull apart easily; serve in tortillas or over Basic Cole Slaw.

Make it your own:
- ✓ Short on time? Use store-bought BBQ sauce instead
- ✓ Top with Taco Sauce (see Dressings, Dips and Sauces) and ¼ avocado per serving

Suggested side dishes:

- **South of the Border Spanish Rice** (see *Sides: starchy carbs*)
- **Black Beans** (canned is OK, just rinse and drain them and heat in a pan with a little hot sauce)
- **Basic Cole Slaw** (see *Sides: Asian Cole Slaw* for recipe)

Whole-Lotta Enchilada

Makes 4 servings

Meat:

~ 1 pound chicken breasts

~ 2 tsp. olive oil

~ 2 tsp. chili powder

~ 1 tsp. cumin

~ ½ tsp. paprika or smoked paprika

Sauce:

~ (1) 14 ½ ounce can diced tomatoes

~ 3 cloves garlic, minced

~ ½ onion, minced

~ ½ tsp. olive oil

~ 2 tsp. chili powder

~ 2 tsp. cumin

~ ¼ tsp. each sea salt and black pepper

Extras:

~ 8 organic corn tortillas

~ 3.8 ounce can sliced black olives, rinsed and drained

~ 2 Tbsp. sliced jalapenos (jarred or fresh)

~ ¼ cup low-fat shredded cheddar cheese

Preheat oven to 350 degrees; dice chicken into very small pieces and cook in pan over medium heat with all meat ingredients until cooked through; meanwhile in another pan, cook onion and garlic in olive oil until onion is translucent, about 5 minutes, then transfer to a food processor with all sauce ingredients and process until smooth; warm tortillas in microwave or pan so they are pliable, and on each tortilla, put chicken, olives, jalapenos and cheese then roll up and place in 9 x 13 inch baking dish, cover with sauce and bake for 15 to 20 minutes; remove from oven and let cool a few minutes before serving.

Make it your own:
- ✓ Short on time? Use jarred salsa instead of making sauce (do NOT use canned enchilada sauce- it has way too much sodium)
- ✓ Still short on time? Make it a casserole: instead of rolling ingredients into each individual tortilla, dump 'em all in the baking dish, top with tortillas and sauce, then bake!
- ✓ Don't like onions, olives, jalapenos, cheese? Leave 'em out
- ✓ Add spinach to enchiladas before rolling up tortillas for more nutrients

Suggested side dishes:
- **South of the Border Spanish Rice** (see *Sides: starchy carbs*)
- **Black Beans** (canned is OK, just rinse and drain them and heat in a pan with a little hot sauce)
- **Basic Cole Slaw** (see *Sides: Asian Cole Slaw* for recipe)

Sunday Meat Sauce

Makes 3 to 4 servings

~ 1 pound ground beef

~ 2 Tbsp. olive oil

~ (1) 28-ounce can unsalted whole, peeled plum tomatoes

~ ¼ onion, chopped

~ 1 to 2 cloves garlic, minced

~ ¼ cup pitted Kalamata olives, finely chopped (jarred in olive oil)

~ 1 Tbsp. sun dried tomatoes, finely chopped (jarred in olive oil)

~ ¼ tsp. each basil, oregano, thyme, rosemary (or use 1 tsp. Italian seasoning)

~ ¼ tsp. each sea salt, black pepper, garlic powder

Cook meat in a pan with 1 Tbsp. olive oil. In another pot, cook onion and garlic with 1 Tbsp. olive oil until onion is translucent then add tomatoes (squish them in your hand as you put them in to break 'em up), add ½ cup water and remaining ingredients; stir to combine, bring to a boil then simmer on low heat 15 to 20 minutes. Add cooked meat to sauce and serve over your favorite pasta.

Make it your own:
✓ For a smoother sauce, pulse all ingredients (except beef and olive oil) in a food processor before heating

> ✓ For Arrabbiata (spicy) sauce, add crushed red pepper flakes to taste before heating
> ✓ Don't like olives or onions? Leave 'em out!
> ✓ Save your leftover sauce and meat to make chili or stuffed peppers with! (See One-Plate Wonders for recipes)

Suggested side dishes:

- This would be great over any **favorite pasta**, we use quinoa pasta for a gluten free option
- You could also do this over cooked **spaghetti squash**: puncture squash with a sharp knife a few times, heat in microwave 10 to 12 minutes, let cool 5 minutes then cut in half and scrape the flesh out.
- **Garlic bread** is a given here! We use gluten free bread topped with olive oil, fresh garlic (or garlic powder), rosemary, dash of salt and sometimes a sprinkle of parmesan cheese, then heat under the broiler until browned
- **Side Salad 101** or **Krazy Kale Salad** would be a great starter (see *Sides* for recipes)
- And a **glass of wine**, of course!

ALL-IN-ONE'S

(NO SIDES NEEDED)

ENTRÉE SALADS

Tasty Taco Salad
Makes 2 servings

Meat:

~ 1 ¼ lb. package lean ground turkey or beef*

~ 1 bell pepper (any color), diced

~ 1 tsp. each: garlic powder, oregano, paprika, cumin, black pepper

~ ½ tsp. sea salt

~ 1 Tbsp. olive oil

Salad:

~ 4 cups mixed lettuce

~ 1 tomato, diced

~ ½ avocado, diced

~ Tasty Taco Topper or Colonel Mustard dressing (see *Dressings, Dips and Sauces*)

Put all meat ingredients in a pan with olive oil and cook over medium heat, chopping up meat into small pieces until cooked through.

Put salad ingredients on 2 plates; divide meat into 4 or 5 servings (depending on how many ounces you want) and put on top of lettuce; top with dressing of choice.

This makes more meat than you will need for this recipe so save the rest for lunch or dinner tomorrow, maybe a burrito or chili!

Make it your own:
- ✓ Chicken, tilapia or salmon are great on this instead of turkey or beef; just cook it up with the same seasonings
- ✓ Don't feel like making dressing? Top your salad off with some salsa!
- ✓ Add any of your favorite veggies- corn would be great, too!
- ✓ Serve with **Corn Tortilla Chips** (see Hummus recipe in Dressings, Dips and Sauces section)

Da Bomb BBQ Chicken Salad

Makes 2 servings

~ 1 pound chicken breasts (you will have leftovers depending on your serving size)

~ ½ cup BBQ Sauce *(see Dressings, Dips and Sauces)*

~ ½ cup corn (frozen or canned*)

~ ½ cup black beans (canned*)

~ ½ red bell pepper, diced

~ 2 Tbsp. red onion, diced

~ 4 cups mixed lettuce

~ ½ avocado, diced

~ 2 Tbsp. fresh cilantro, chopped

~ Ranch dressing or Taco Sauce *(see Dressings, Dips and Sauces)*

  * *Rinse and drain canned corn and beans*

Cut chicken into 1-inch cubes and cook in a pan with BBQ sauce until cooked through; meanwhile, in another pan heat corn, beans, bell pepper and onion until warmed through; put lettuce on 2 plates, top with chicken and bean mix, avocado, cilantro and dressing and serve.

> **Make it your own:**
> ✓ Add or subtract veggies as you like
> ✓ Add hot sauce to your bean mix if you like it spicy
> ✓ The bean mix would be great in tacos, too!
> ✓ Top with crushed **Brown Rice Tortilla Chips** (see Hummus recipe in Dressings, Dips and Sauces section)

'Get-Your-Greek-On' Salad with Chicken

Makes 2 servings

Meat:

~ 1 pound chicken breasts (you will have leftovers
   depending on your serving size)

~ 1 Tbsp. olive oil

~ ½ tsp. oregano

~ ½ tsp. black pepper

~ ¼ tsp. sea salt

Salad:

~ 4 cups Romaine lettuce, chopped into bite-size pieces

~ 1 cucumber, diced

~ 1 tomato, diced

~ 1/3 cup Kalamata olives

~ few slices red onion

Dressing:

~ 2 tsp. lemon juice

~ 2 Tbsp. olive oil

Put all meat ingredients in a pan with olive oil and cook until cooked through; put salad ingredients on 2 plates and top with chicken; whisk lemon juice and olive oil together, drizzle over salad and serve.

Short on time? Cut the chicken into small cubes or strips before cooking- they'll cook faster!

Build-Your-Own Salads

It's easy to put together a great entrée salad with foods you already have in your kitchen. Just pick one or more item from each category and build your own custom creation!

Choose your greens:

mixed greens   Romaine

spinach   kale

Choose your toppings:

Fruit: apples   berries

avocado   grapes

Veggies:

artichokes   tomatoes   corn

peppers   cucumber   celery

carrots   olives   onions

Nuts and seeds:

almonds   walnuts

pecans   pumpkin seeds

cashews   sunflower seeds

Choose your protein:

grilled chicken   ground turkey or beef

grilled fish   fresh deli meats (no nitrites added)

canned tuna (rinsed and drained)

canned salmon (rinsed and drained)

Any of the *Main Protein* recipes or *Entrée Salad* proteins would work here too.

Choose your dressing:

See *Dressings, Dips and Sauces*

ONE-PLATE WONDERS

'Jack Talk Thai' Chicken Bowl

Makes 2 servings

Meat:

~ 1 pound chicken breasts (you will have leftovers
   depending on your serving size)

~ 2 Tbsp. peanut butter (or almond butter)

~ 1 Tbsp. soy sauce (or tamari or coconut aminos)

~ 2 tsp. honey

~ ¼ cup almond milk (or coconut milk)

~ hot sauce to taste (we like Sriracha with this dish)

Extras:

~ 2 cups mixed veggies (broccoli, carrots, cauliflower; most
   stores have pre-packaged)

~ ½ cup cooked brown rice (cook according to package or
   buy pre-cooked package, available at stores like Trader
   Joe's) or ½ cup cooked quinoa.

Dice chicken into 1-inch cubes, combine with all meat ingredients
and cook in pan over medium heat until cooked through;
meanwhile steam veggies: put them in a pan with a little water,
cover and cook over medium heat until softened, about 10
minutes; divide cooked rice between 2 plates, top with veggies,
chicken and sauce.

Spicy Italian Stuffed Peppers

Makes 4 stuffed halves; 1 to 2 halves is 1 serving

Meat:

~ 1 pound lean ground turkey or beef

~ 2 Tbsp. olive oil

~ 2 Tbsp. onion, diced

~ 1 clove garlic, minced

~ ¼ cup tomato sauce (or 1 Tbsp. tomato paste plus 3 Tbsp. water)

~ ¼ tsp. each basil, oregano, thyme, rosemary (or use 1 tsp. Italian seasoning)

~ ¼ tsp. each sea salt, black pepper, garlic powder, paprika

~ 1 tsp. crushed red chili flakes

Extras:

~ 2 bell peppers (any color)

~ ½ cup cooked quinoa (see *Sides* for recipe)

~ 2 cups spinach

~ 2 Tbsp. parmesan cheese

Cut bell peppers in half (top to bottom), remove seeds and stem and place cut side down in a pan with a little water, cover and cook on medium heat about 10 minutes. Meanwhile in another pan with olive oil, cook all the meat ingredients, breaking up the meat into small pieces and cook until browned and cooked through. Add quinoa and spinach and cook until spinach cooks down, stir to combine. Place peppers cut side up in an oven-safe dish, stuff each half with ¼ of the meat mixture and top with parmesan cheese. Place under oven broiler to melt cheese, about 2 to 4 minutes; serve.

Make it your own:

✓ Watching your carb intake? Leave out the quinoa and add extra spinach

✓ Make 'em Spanish peppers by adding ¼ cup salsa to the meat sauce and top with cheddar or cotija cheese instead of parmesan

✓ Use your leftover Chili or Sunday Meat Sauce here – just add the quinoa and spinach to it, heat it up, then stuff your peppers!

Zucchini "Pasta" with Chicken and Pine Nuts

Makes 2 servings

Meat:

~ 1 pound chicken breasts, cut into 1-inch cubes (you will have leftovers depending on your serving size)

~ 1 Tbsp olive oil

~ ¼ tsp. each basil, oregano, thyme, rosemary (or use 1 tsp. Italian seasoning)

~ ¼ tsp. each sea salt, black pepper, garlic powder

~ ½ tsp. crushed red pepper flakes

~ 2 Tbsp. sundried tomatoes

~ 2 Tbsp. pine nuts

Extras:

~ 4 medium zucchini

~ ½ tsp. olive oil

~ 2 Tbsp. fresh grated parmesan

Cook all meat ingredients in a pan with olive oil on medium heat until meat is cooked through; meanwhile, cut the ends off the zucchini and cut into very thin slices, then cut slices into thin "noodles;" saute zucchini in another pan with olive oil just until soft and slightly browned; put zucchini on a plate, top with meat and sprinkle with parmesan; serve.

Meaty Black Bean Chili

Makes 3 to 4 servings

~ 1 Tbsp. olive oil

~ 1 pound lean ground beef

~ ¼ tsp. each sea salt and pepper

~½ onion, finely diced

~ 2 cloves garlic, finely diced

~ ½ red bell pepper, finely diced

~ ½ jalapeno, seeded and finely diced

~ 3 tsp. chili powder

~ ½ tsp. cumin

~ (1) 28-ounce can diced tomatoes, no salt added

~ ¾ cup chicken or beef broth/stock

~ 1 cup canned black beans, rinsed and drained

Cook meat in pan with olive oil, salt and pepper over medium heat, breaking into small pieces as it cooks, until cooked through; add onion, garlic, red bell pepper, jalapeno, chili powder and cumin, cook for 5 minutes then add diced tomatoes (and juices) and broth; cook until it bubbles then add beans and cook for another 15 minutes; let cool slightly and serve.

Make it your own:
- ✓ Use ground turkey or finely diced chicken breast instead of beef
- ✓ Add 2 cups of spinach during the last 15 minutes cooking time for more nutrients
- ✓ Add Tabasco if you like it spicier

> ✓ For a *really* easy, time-saving version of chili, save your meat sauce from Sunday, add chicken or beef broth, cumin, black beans and jarred salsa!
>
> ✓ Save your leftover chili to make **Stuffed Peppers** with! (see recipe in this section)

Suggested side dishes:

- **Side Salad 101** or **Krazy Kale Salad** would be a great starter (see *Sides*)

- **Brown Rice Tortilla Chips** would be great for some crunch (see Hummus recipe in *Dressings, Dips and Sauces* section)

Loaded Baked Potato

Makes 2 to 4 servings

~ 2 medium russet potatoes

~ 8 to 16 ounces prepared protein*

~ 2 Tbsp. light sour cream or light cream cheese

~ 1 cup prepared vegetables of choice

Clean potatoes and puncture a few times with a fork; microwave about 8 minutes or until soft and remove (be careful, they will be very hot!); cut a lengthwise slit in each potato, top with sour cream or cream cheese, stuff with veggies and microwave another 2 minutes until veggies are warmed.

* Any of the Main Meal Proteins would be great here, or if you don't have any prepared, top it with canned tuna (rinsed and drained).

Make it your own:
- ✓ Any veggies would work here, even frozen! Or top it with a handful of spinach
- ✓ Top with salsa or hot sauce for more flavor
- ✓ Make this ahead of time and pack it to-go! Just reheat it in the microwave!

HEALTHY ENTERTAINING AND INDULGENCES

APPETIZERS

Company Crab Cakes

Makes 4 servings as an appetizer, 2 as a main protein*

- ~ 12 ounces lump crab meat
- ~ 3 Tbsp. onion, minced
- ~ 1 egg
- ~ 3 Tbsp. red bell pepper, minced
- ~ 3 Tbsp. low-fat mayonnaise or plain Greek yogurt
- ~ ¼ tsp. each paprika, cayenne pepper, garlic powder, sea salt, black pepper
- ~ 4 Tbsp. almond meal
- ~ 1 Tbsp. olive oil

Mix all ingredients until combined; shape into about 3-inch diameter patties and cook in pan with olive oil until golden on each side. Serve with a side of **Colonel Mustard Dressing** *(see Dressings, Dips and Sauces).*

*This would be great as a Main Meal Protein over one of the salads!

Smoked Salmon Pate

Makes about 12 ounces

~ 4 ounces flaked smoked salmon

~ 8 ounces fat-free cream cheese

~ 2 Tbsp. fresh chives, minced

~ 3 Tbsp. fresh dill, minced

~ 3 Tbsp. lemon juice

~ dash hot sauce

In a food processor, mix half the salmon and all remaining ingredients until smooth; transfer to a serving bowl and mix in remaining salmon; cover and refrigerate a few hours to chill. Serve with crackers, or small pieces of toasted bread (crostini).

Caprese Skewers

Make as many as needed

~ cherry or grape tomatoes

~ fresh basil leaves

~ fresh mozzarella balls

~ extra virgin olive oil

~ balsamic vinegar

~ salt and pepper

~ toothpicks

On each toothpick, stack a small basil leaf (skewer at one end of the basil), one tomato, one piece mozzarella (about the same size as the tomato) and then hook the other end of the basil on the end of the toothpick so it makes a "cradle" for the cheese and tomato. Place on a plate, drizzle with olive oil and balsamic and sprinkle a little salt and pepper. Make about 4 to 5 skewers per person. (This makes a great presentation to take to parties, too!)

Popeye's Poppers

Makes 16 to 18 poppers

~ (1) 14-ounce can artichoke hearts, drained and finely chopped

~ 10 ounces frozen spinach, thawed and drained*

~ ¼ cup shredded mozzarella cheese

~ 6 eggs, whites only

~ 1 clove garlic, minced

~ ½ tsp. oregano

~ ¼ tsp. sea salt

~ ½ tsp. black pepper

Preheat oven to 350 degrees; mix all ingredients, spray a mini-muffin pan with cooking spray and fill with popper batter; bake 25 to 30 minutes, then serve.

* You may need to lay out the spinach in paper towels and squeeze the excess water out if it's too wet.

Yep, There's More!

- **Hummus** or **Cucumber Yogurt Dip** would be great served with fresh cut veggies, crackers or pita.
- Put out a small bowl of nuts and olives
- Grapes and a variety of cheeses with crackers

DESSERTS

24-Carrot Cupcakes

Makes 6 cupcakes

~ 2 large or 3 medium carrots, shredded

~ 1/3 cup unsweetened applesauce

~ 2 tsp. honey, agave or coconut nectar

~ 1 Tbsp. coconut milk

~ 2 eggs, whites only

~ 1 tsp. vanilla extract

~ ¼ cup flour (or gluten-free flour)

~ 1/3 cup almond meal

~ ½ tsp. baking soda

~ ¼ tsp. sea salt

~ ½ tsp. cinnamon

~ 1/8 tsp. ground allspice

~ ¼ cup unsweetened shredded coconut

Preheat oven to 350 degrees. Mix all together in a bowl; pour into muffin pan sprayed with cooking spray, fill each about ½ full and bake for about 15 minutes or until tops are golden and muffins are cooked through. Top each with frosting just before serving.

Frosting: stir together ¼ cup low-fat cream cheese, 2 tsp. honey and ½ tsp. vanilla extract.

Chocolate Nut Clusters*

Makes 10 to 12

~ ½ cup almonds

~ 4 ounces 70% cacao dark chocolate bar or dark chocolate
    chips

Melt chocolate in a pan over low heat or in a microwave-safe bowl; stir in almonds; drop by spoonful onto foil-lined plate and keep in fridge until ready to serve.

Make 'em Almond Joy Clusters by stirring in ¼ cup shredded coconut!

Chocolate Truffles

Makes about 6 truffles

~ ¼ cup uncooked oatmeal

~ 1 tsp. cinnamon

~ ¼ cup cocoa powder

~ 2 tsp. honey, agave or coconut nectar

~ 1 cup pitted dates

~ ¼ cup walnuts, chopped

Mix oats, cinnamon and cocoa in a food processor or blender to combine then add sweetener and dates and mix until a stiff dough forms (add a few spoonfuls water if mix is too dry); mix in walnuts by hand and form into small balls, wet hands if dough is too sticky. Roll in cocoa powder if desired. Store in fridge or freezer.

Spicy Oatmeal Walnut Cookies

Makes 24 cookies

~ 1 cup rolled oats (to process into flour) plus

~ 1 ½ cups rolled oats

~ 1 ½ tsp. baking soda

~ 1 tsp. cinnamon

~ ½ tsp. nutmeg

~ ½ tsp. ground ginger

~ ¼ tsp. sea salt

~ ½ cup honey

~ 2/3 cup applesauce (unsweetened)

~ 1 tsp. vanilla extract

~ 1 egg

~ 1 Tbsp. coconut oil, melted

~ ½ cup walnuts (chopped)

Preheat oven to 350 degrees. In a food processor, combine 1 cup flour, baking soda, cinnamon, nutmeg, ginger and salt until ground to a soft flour; transfer to a large bowl and stir in remaining ingredients until well blended; spoon out cookie dough onto a foil-lined baking sheet sprayed with cooking spray; bake about 10 minutes until golden. Remove from oven and let cool about 10 minutes before serving.

Make it your own:
✓ Substitute chocolate chips or dried cranberries/blueberries for the walnuts

Apple Crisps (see *Snacks, Shakes & Desserts* for recipe) would be a great option for dessert here, too! Use as many apples as needed for your number of guests and increase ingredients accordingly; you could bake it in a casserole dish and scoop out each serving or bake in individual small bowls.

COCKTAILS AND MOCKTAILS

Berry Mojitos
Makes 2 servings

~ 3 ounces light rum

~ ¼ cup fresh or frozen berries, any kind

~ 5 fresh mint leaves

~ 1 ounce lime juice

~ ½ ounce agave or honey

~ splash club soda

Put berries, mint and lime juice in a shaker and muddle it (smash it all together) then add rum, sweetener and ice and shake well; pour into 2 glasses and top with club soda.

Make it a Mocktail by leaving out the rum.

Grapefruit Splash
Makes 2 servings

~ 3 ounces vodka

~ 3 ounces grapefruit juice (unsweetened)

~ 5 ounces club soda

Put all in a glass over ice and stir, enjoy!

Make it a Mocktail by leaving out the vodka.

Skinny Margarita

Makes 2 servings

~ 3 ounces tequila

~ 1 ounce lime juice*

~ ½ ounce agave or honey

~ splash club soda

Put tequila, lime and agave in a shaker with ice and shake well; pour into 2 glasses and top with club soda.

* Make it a Grapefruit Margarita by using 2 ounces unsweetened grapefruit juice instead of lime juice.

Ginger Spritzer

Makes 2 servings

~ 3 ounces vodka

~ ¼ tsp. fresh grated ginger

~ ½ tsp. agave or honey

~ 8 ounces club soda

Put ginger and sweetener in a cup, add a little club soda and swirl to combine; divide in 2 glasses, add ice and top with club soda and 1 ½ ounces of vodka each.

Make it a Mocktail by leaving out the vodka.

EATING OUT GUIDE

There will undoubtedly be times you will go out to eat so we want to show you how to make good choices while eating out, not just a home.

Above all, you will need to modify what's on the menu. There is rarely a time where we order a dish exactly as it is on the menu. Get used to asking for your food the way you want it; most restaurants are very accommodating to dietary requests.

Always ask: Ask how a dish is prepared and what's in it if you are unsure, so you know exactly what you're getting. Ask for items that aren't on the menu, too. We've eaten out and asked for gluten-free pancakes even though it wasn't on the menu and they had it!

Appetizer items make great entrées, as most entrée dishes are much more than one serving. We usually share an appetizer and an entrée instead of each getting an entrée—it's just too much food.

Salads are good options as well, just be sure to get the dressing on the side or ask for oil and vinegar instead.

Make up your own meal! We often ask for a sandwich without the bread and ask for lots of salad instead. Or order a salad and have them add a grilled chicken breast or fish.

Avoid the obvious fattening choices like items with terms such as: fried, battered, butter, cream and alfredo.

If you don't want starchy carbs with your meal (like potatoes, rice, etc.) ask for extra veggies or salad instead.

Most restaurants use a lot of salt (and I mean a LOT!) It's usually a good idea to get sauces on the side or leave them out entirely, as that's where a lot of the sodium comes from, and be sure to drink a lot of water to flush out all the extra sodium you'll be eating.

We know there will be special occasions where you will want to order a dish exactly as it is on the menu, and that's fine once in a while, just not every time. And if you must have dessert, pick one and share it. Once you find the portions and foods that work for you—the foods that make you your happiest, healthiest and harmonious—you won't want to stray too far from that because you won't like the way you feel when you do.

Here's to health and happiness on your journey of life.

~ Heather and Joe

Disclaimer: This book is designed to provide information about the subject matter. While the publisher and authors have used their best efforts in preparing this book, they make no representations or warranties with respect to the accuracy or completeness of the contents in this book. The views and opinions expressed in this book are strictly those of the author. The advice and strategies contained herein may not be suitable to your situation. This is not intended to replace the advice of your health care provider; please consult a professional for any concerns as to how this relates to your individual situation.

36913796R00064

Made in the USA
Charleston, SC
20 December 2014